AF264378

It's Not Your Fault
was lovingly created and dedicated
just for YOU!

It's not your fault that Mommy's gone
It's hard to understand
But Mom got sick, it's no one's fault
That death took Mommy's hand

Now she's in another place
where she's not sick at all
But where she went, she has to stay
She can't come back at all

She can no longer speak or eat
Play games she used to play
She can no longer walk or talk
Her body's gone away

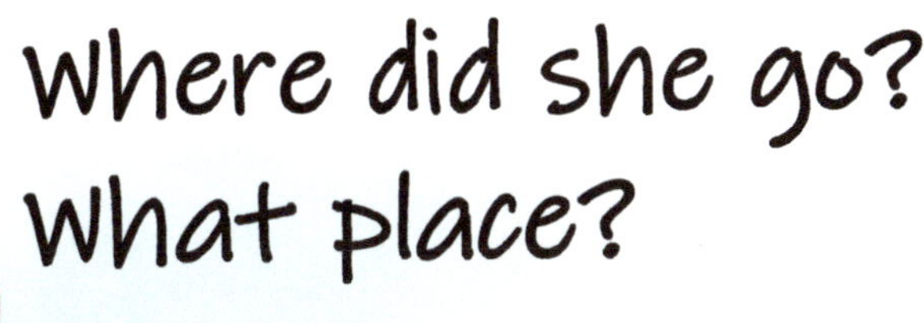

where did she go?
What place?

And how and
where?

Is it a cave
or mountain top?

On land
or in the air?

Some people call it Heaven
Others, Shangri-la
It's an unknown Kingdom
A place of calm and awe

Mom didn't want to go away
She didn't wish to leave you
And if she could she'd still be here
To love and never grieve you

But being sad or mad or scared
Isn't odd or strange
Asking questions, feeling confused
Is normal but will change

Even though Mom has died
There's something else that's true
You'll never **EVER** be alone
Cause I'll take care of you

It's not your fault that Mommy died
Not in any way
It's no one's fault
No one's to blame
I really have to say

She didn't die 'cause you played outside
And got your clothes all dirty
Or jumped or fooled around in bed
Or woke up extra early

It wasn't 'cause you spilled your milk
Or drew pictures on the wall
Or broke a toy
Or skipped your prayers
None of that at all!

Mom didn't die 'cause you got mad
Or yelled at her one day
It wasn't cause you wished she'd die
That made her go away

Moms know we sometimes think or say
Mean things when we are mad
She knew you loved her very much
And she was very glad

She loved you more than all the world
More than the stars or sun
More than the moon up in the sky
Almost more than anyone

Mom would say it's good to cry
When your heart is aching
Sometimes you're going to feel so sad
You'll think your heart is breaking

Other times you'll laugh and play
The sadness will seem gone
And that is more than okay too
We all must carry on

When you think of mom each day
Even though it makes you sad
She'll live forever in your heart
Soon, you won't feel so bad

We'll see her in your drawings
Or in her prized scrapbook
Remember her at special times
Or in pictures that we took

It's not your fault that Mommy died
But even though she's dead
There'll always be a Mommy bond
Connected by love's thread

'Cause even when somebody dies
They're always in your heart
Just because you cannot see them
Doesn't mean you're far apart

Remember Mommy always
And every time you do
You'll hear her whisper in your heart
Sweetheart...

The Beginning . . .